ON FREEDOM

ON FREEDOM

CASS R. SUNSTEIN

PRINCETON UNIVERSITY PRESS

Princeton & Oxford

Requests for permission to reproduce material from this
work should be sent to permissions@press.princeton.edu

Published by Princeton University Press
41 William Street, Princeton, New Jersey 08540
6 Oxford Street, Woodstock, Oxfordshire OX20 1TR

press.princeton.edu

Library of Congress Control Number: 2018953067
ISBN: 9780691191157

British Library Cataloging-in-Publication Data is available

The illustration on page 40 is courtesy of the USDA Center
for Nutrition Policy and Promotion at ChooseMyPlate.gov

Editorial: Eric Crahan and Pamela Weidman
Production Editorial: Ellen Foos
Jacket and Text Design: Chris Ferrante
Production: Jacquie Poirier
Publicity: James Schneider
Copyeditor: Jay Boggis

This book has been composed in Adobe Text Pro,
Berthold Akzidenz Grotesk, and Alternate Gothic

Printed on acid-free paper. ∞

Printed in the United States of America

10 9 8 7 6 5 4 3 2 1

CONTENTS

ON FREEDOM

BITTEN APPLES

Does freedom of choice promote human well-being? Many people think so. They insist that each of us is the best judge of what will promote our own well-being. They argue that people should be allowed to go their own way, so long as they are not harming others.

But what if people do not know how to find their way? What if they have no idea?

For many of us, *navigability* is a serious problem—perhaps the most serious problem of all. Navigating an unfamiliar city or an airport might be baffling. The same might be true of the health care bureaucracy or the criminal justice system. When life is hard to navigate, people are less free. They are unable to get where they want to go. The challenge arises not only when we are looking for literal destinations (a gasoline station, a bank, a doctor's office), but also when we are seeking some kind of outcome (good health, a visa, a decent place to live, personal safety, economic security, a satisfying relationship, a good job).

Obstacles to navigability are major sources of unfreedom in human life. They create a kind of bondage. They make people feel lost. In wealthy countries and poor ones, they reduce people's well-being. Freedom of choice is important, even critical, but it is undermined or even destroyed if life cannot be navigated. Obstacles to navigability have been the great blind spot in the Western philosophical tradition. They deserve sustained attention—not only from philosophers and political theorists but also from economists, psychologists, designers, architects, computer scientists, lawyers, public officials, the private sector, and ordinary citizens.

Navigability is a particularly difficult challenge when people face problems of self-control. When people cannot overcome those problems, their freedom is badly compromised. Consider smoking, drinking, overeating, gambling, and drug use. Addiction is the most extreme case, but self-control problems are everywhere.[1] A special obstacle to solving those problems is "present bias": people often focus on today and not tomorrow, which means that they will choose short-term pleasure and avoid short-term pain, even when that choice makes their lives worse (and less meaningful). At the same time, people often know that that they are making a mistake. They want help. They seek to find the right path. With modest interventions, people can solve self-control problems—and do so while retaining their freedom (and from a certain point of view, even increasing it).

While my main focus is on navigability, I shall also be asking these questions about freedom and well-being: *What if people's free choices are decisively influenced by some aspect of the social environment, and they are happy either way? In such cases, how should designers of the social environment—employers, teachers, doctors, investment advisers, companies, governments—proceed?* As we shall see, these questions are both difficult and fundamental.

In almost everyone's life, some free choice has made all the difference—even if that choice was the product of serendipity, or a small or seemingly accidental factor. At the last minute, you might have taken one course in high school rather than another, and the teacher changed the course of your life. On a lark, you might have gone to a party that you dreaded, and you happened to catch someone's eye. That someone is now your spouse. Or some work commitment was cancelled, and so you visited a city, far away, to spend a little time with a friend. To your amazement, you fell in love with the place. It is now your home.

Writers of science fiction (along with some philosophers and historians) like to speak of "parallel worlds" or "counterfactual history." I am focusing on something similar and narrower: cases in which some feature of the social environment leads people to choose Option A, Option B, Option C, or Option D—and choosers end up glad after the fact, never wishing things should be different, *whatever they chose*.

Some such cases are fairly mundane. For example, we can imagine situations in which people would be content with one or another health care plan, and what they choose is a product of a seemingly innocuous social cue (such as a font or color on a website). Other cases involve large features of people's lives—situations in which people would be content with one or another city, spouse, or career—and a seemingly innocuous social cue (an advertisement, a smile, a word of encouragement, a path of least resistance) makes all the difference. In the hardest cases, where free choices can lead in different directions, there is no escape from evaluating outcomes by asking about what promotes people's well-being. At least there is no escape from that question if a designer of the social environment—an employer, a doctor, a government—is deciding what kind of social environment to design.

A STRANGE NEW SMELL

Two passages will help frame the discussion. The first should be familiar:

So when the woman saw that the tree was good for food, and that it was a delight to the eyes, and that the tree was to be desired to make one wise, she took of its fruit and ate; and she also gave some to her husband, who was with her, and he ate.

Then the eyes of both were opened, and they knew that they were naked; and they sewed fig leaves together and made loincloths for themselves.[2]

The second passage is from a magnificent novel on the topic of freedom, A. S. Byatt's *Possession* (1990), after a fateful choice (and yes, it involved a love affair):

In the morning, the whole world had a strange new smell. It was the smell of the aftermath, a green smell, a smell of shredded leaves and oozing resin, of crushed wood and splashed sap, a tart smell, which bore some relation to the smell of bitten apples. It was the smell of death and destruction, and it smelled fresh and lively and hopeful.[3]

In *Genesis*, Adam and Eve exercised their freedom of choice, and everything was lost. (Much was gained as well.) Byatt is also speaking of a free choice and a kind of fall. Although her tale overlaps with that of *Genesis*, her account is far more upbeat. There is a smell of death and destruction, but it is full of life and hope. Let us be clear: Every human being is blessed to experience that smell.

Do people's free choices really make their lives go better? The liberal philosophical tradition offers a simple answer: *Yes.*[4] Artists, novelists, psychologists, and theologians offer a more complicated answer, and they are right to insist that the simple answer is far too simple.

People might have no idea how to get where they want to go. Like Adam and Eve, they can be tempted. Sometimes they lack self-control. Background conditions greatly matter. Sometimes people's choices are not, in the deepest sense, their own; they are deprived, deceived, or manipulated. Sometimes people lack crucial information. Sometimes their preferences are a product of injustice or deprivation. Sometimes they simply blunder. As a result, their lives go much worse.

To make progress, I will focus largely on what Richard Thaler and I call "nudges":[5] interventions that steer people in certain directions, but that also preserve freedom of choice. But I shall have something to say about coercion as well.

The topic of navigability does not, of course, come anywhere close to exhausting the topic of freedom. I will not, for example, explore the differences between "negative freedom" and "positive freedom"; say a word about freedom of speech and freedom of religion; make a final judgment about John Stuart Mill's Harm Principle;[6] or investigate the claim that property rights, conferred by the state, can be essential to freedom, or an abridgement of freedom. My hope is that my tighter focus can offer some new perspectives on both the human condition and enduring problems, some of which are especially pressing in the current period.

CHAPTER 1

WHAT THE HELL IS WATER?

Here is a tale from the novelist David Foster Wallace: "There are these two young fish swimming along and they happen to meet an older fish swimming the other way, who nods at them and says 'Morning, boys. How's the water?' And the two young fish swim on for a bit, and then eventually one of them looks over at the other and goes 'What the hell is water?' "[1]

This is a tale about *choice architecture*—the environment in which choices are made. Choice architecture is inevitable, whether or not we see it, and it affects our choices. It is the equivalent of water. Weather is itself a form of choice architecture, because it influences what people decide. On snowy days, for example, people are especially likely to purchase cars with four-wheel drive, which they do not always love, and return to the market unusually quickly.[2] Human beings cannot live without some kind of weather. Nature provides a kind of choice architecture. So do people in both public and private sectors. The law of contract is a regulatory system, and it influences us, even if it gives us a great deal of flexibility and preserves a lot of space for freedom of choice. For example, contract law includes "default rules," which specify what happens if the contract is silent on a disputed question. Because contracts are often silent, default rules can make all the difference.

We can insist on freedom of choice all we like, but we cannot wish choice architecture away. Any store, real or online, must have a design; some products are seen first, and others are seen last, and still others are barely seen at all. Any menu places options at various locations. Television stations are assigned different numbers, and strikingly, the number matters, even when the costs of switching are vanishingly low; people tend to choose stations with lower numbers.[3] Any website has a design, which will affect what and whether people will choose. One of the best books on website design is entitled *Don't Make Me Think*.[4] The title signals the importance of navigability. It suggests that the best websites are so easy to navigate that you don't even know that you are navigating them.

It would be possible, of course, to define choice architecture in a narrow way, and to limit it to intentional designs by human beings. There is nothing intrinsic to human language that rules out that definition, and my emphasis here will be on intentional design. But if the goal is to see how and when people are influenced, the broader definition is preferable. It shows that our choices are often an artifact of an architecture for which no human being may have responsibility—a sunny day, an un-expected chill, a gust of wind, a steep hill, a full (and romantic) moon.

NUDGES

Nudges are interventions that fully preserve freedom of choice, but that also steer people's decisions in certain directions. In daily life, a GPS device is an example of a nudge. It re-spects your freedom; you can ignore its ad-vice if you like. Perhaps you like a more scenic route; perhaps you enjoy seeing familiar land-marks. But the device is there to help you to get to your preferred destination. It increases navigability.

Many other nudges have a similar goal. Signs are nudges. So are calorie labels at restaurants;

text messages, informing customers that a bill is due or that a doctor's appointment is scheduled for the next day; automatic enrollment in pension plans; default settings on computers and cell phones; and programs for automatic payment of credit card bills and mortgages. In government, nudges include graphic warnings for cigarettes; mandatory labels for energy efficiency or fuel economy; "nutrition facts" panels on food; and automatic enrollment in benefits programs. All of these are forms of choice architecture. Whatever form of choice architecture is in place, it will nudge.

Those who favor nudges emphasize that human beings often lack important information, have limited attention, face self-control problems, and suffer from behavioral biases. We have already encountered "present bias." People may also procrastinate; for many of us, inertia is a powerful force. We are often unrealistically optimistic and overconfident, and we may either exaggerate or underestimate serious risks. In these circumstances, nudges can be exceedingly helpful. They can improve the lives of people who lack information or suffer from behavioral biases, without harming those who do not. A key reason is that nudges make life more navigable.

Many policies, by contrast, take the form of *mandates* and *bans*. For example, criminal law forbids theft and assault. It does not allow people to go their own way. Other policies take the form of *economic incentives* (including disincentives), such as subsidies for renewable fuels, fees for engaging in certain activities, or taxes on gasoline and tobacco products. These policies play important roles, but they are not nudges. Mandates and bans eliminate freedom of choice, at least in the sense that they are meant as flat prohibitions. Incentives maintain freedom of choice, but they impose a kind of skew. If nudges do that as well, it is not because they impose material burdens or grant material benefits.

In recent years, a primary goal of behaviorally informed policy has been to insist that many interventions, both private and public, are forms of choice architecture that decisively affect choices and outcomes, even if they do not alter incentives. Because of the appeal of choice-preserving approaches, many nations have shown keen interest in nudges and nudging, and have established Nudge Units, or Behavioral Insights Teams, to promote health and safety or otherwise to help fulfill important goals.[5] By any measure, the consequences of some nudges are not properly described as modest—in the United States, the United Kingdom, the Netherlands, Ireland, Denmark, Singapore, and numerous other nations.

Because of automatic enrollment in free school meals programs, more than 10 million poor American children are now receiving free breakfast and lunch during the school year. With respect to savings, automatic enrollment in pension programs has produced massive increases in participation rates.[6] Credit card legislation, enacted in 2010, is saving consumers more than $10 billion annually; significant portions of those savings come from nudges and nudgelike interventions.[7]

Other nudges, now in early stages or under discussion, could also have a major impact. The Earned Income Tax Credit is among the most effective antipoverty programs in the world, but many eligible people do not take advantage of it. Automatic enrollment would have large consequences for the lives of millions of people. In many nations, automatic voter registration would turn countless people into eligible voters. If the goal is to reduce green-house gas emissions, automatic enrollment in green energy would have large effects.

With respect to the world's most serious problems (including relief of poverty, reduction of violence, and improvement of health), the use of nudges remains in its preliminary stages. We will see far more in the future, and the impact will not be small. The point to underline here is that nudges insist that people should be free to choose. If they do not like the direction in which they are being nudged, they can choose to go where they like.

FEAR OF GOVERNMENT

Many people object to nudges for one reason above all: fear of government. Suppose that public officials are incompetent, self-interested, reckless, or corrupt. Suppose that your least favorite leaders are or will be in charge. Would you want them to nudge? If interest groups are able to push government in their preferred directions, and if public officials lack crucial information, then you might insist: Do not nudge! Reliance on private markets might seem far better.

Indeed, behavioral science itself might be taken to put this conclusion in bold letters. There is no reason to think that public officials are immune to behavioral biases. In a democratic society, the electoral connection might mean that they will respond to the same biases that affect ordinary people. To be sure, structural safeguards might help, especially if they are designed to promote reflection and deliberation, and if they ensure a large role for technocrats who are insistent on science and on careful attention to costs and benefits. But in any real-world polity, behavioral distortions are difficult to avoid.

These are fair and important points. But as we have seen, they run into a logical problem: a great deal of nudging is inevitable. So long as government has offices and websites, it will be nudging. If the law establishes contract, property, and tort law, it will be nudging, if only because it will set out default rules, which establish what happens if people do nothing. Friedrich Hayek, the greatest critic of socialism, wrote that the task of establishing a competitive system provides "a wide and unquestioned field for state activity," for "in no system that could be rationally defended would the state just do nothing. An effective competitive system needs an intelligently designed and continuously adjusted legal framework as much as any other."[8]

As Hayek understood, a state that protects private property and that enforces contracts has to establish a set of prohibitions and permissions, including a set of default entitlements, establishing who has what before bargaining begins. If government is up and running, that is just the tip of the iceberg. For that reason, it is pointless to exclaim, "do not nudge!"—at least if one does not embrace anarchy.

Because nudges maintain freedom of choice, they offer a safety valve against official error. Those who favor nudges do not trust government. On the contrary, they are keenly alert to the possibility that public officials will show behavioral biases or otherwise make mistakes. For those who fear or distrust government, the principal focus should be on mandates, bans, subsidies, and taxes. To be sure, nudges ought not to be free from scrutiny.

It is true, of course, that some nudging is optional. Government can warn people about smoking, opioid addiction, and distracted driving, or not. It can seek to protect consumers against deception and manipulation, or not. It can undertake public education campaigns, or not. If you think that government is entirely untrustworthy, you might want it to avoid nudging whenever it can.

In the abstract, that position cannot be ruled out of bounds. On highly pessimistic assumptions about the capacities and incentives of public officials, and highly optimistic assumptions about the capacities and incentives of those in the private sector, official nudging should be minimized. But private actors nudge, and sometimes it is very much in their interest to exploit behavioral biases, thus causing serious harm to countless people. Would it be a terrific idea to forbid public officials from taking steps to reduce smoking and distracted driving? In any case, the track record of real-world nudging includes impressive success stories, certainly if success is measured by cost-effectiveness. Sometimes nudges turn out to be the best tools of all.[9]

Everyone should agree that government nudges, like other official interventions, should be constrained by democratic requirements, including transparency, public debate, and independent monitoring (including continuing evaluation of how nudges work in practice). Nudging must also be respectful of individual rights. Constraints of this kind can reduce the risks (without eliminating them). The fundamental point is that those risks are far larger with other tools, above all mandates and bans.

AS JUDGED BY THEMSELVES

Some nudges are designed to reduce negative externalities, understood as harmful effects on third parties; consider fuel economy labels that draw attention to environmental consequences, or default rules that automatically enroll people in green energy. Nudges can easily be designed to reduce theft, assault, and rape. But many nudges are designed *to increase the likelihood that people's choices will improve their own well-being.* In such cases, the central goal of nudging is to "make choosers better off, *as judged by themselves.*"[10]

That idea borrows from the liberal philosophical tradition in the sense that it gives ultimate authority to individual choosers. It makes them sovereign. It respects their dignity and their freedom. For reasons that may involve autonomy or that may involve well-being, it allows them to have the final say. I will be focusing much of the discussion here on the "as judged by themselves" criterion and attempting to explore its complexities. As we shall see, navigability is a crucial part of the picture.

Social planners in government—or in the terminology that Richard Thaler and I prefer, *choice architects*—might well have their own ideas about what would make choosers better off. But in general, the lodestar is people's own judgments. A central reason is that human well-being matters, and those judgments are a reasonable (if imperfect) way to test the question of whether nudges are promoting their well-being.

It should be clear that this claim places a premium on human agency. It builds on the view, associated with John Stuart Mill, that individuals are in a unique position to know what will improve their well-being, and that outsiders will often blunder. Mill insists that the individual "is the person most interested in his own well-being," and the "ordinary man or woman has means of knowledge immeasurably surpassing those that can be possessed by any one else."[11] When society seeks to overrule the individual's judgment, it does so on the basis of "general presumptions," and these "may be altogether wrong, and even if right, are as likely as not to be misapplied to individual cases." If the goal is to ensure that people's lives go well,

Mill concludes that the best solution is for public officials to allow people to find their own path. Consider in the same vein F. A. Hayek's remarkable suggestion that "the awareness of our irremediable ignorance of most of what is known to somebody [who is the chooser] is *the chief basis of the argument for liberty*."[12]

To be sure, behavioral science raises questions about these claims insofar as it finds that human beings often make decisions that impair their own well-being. Some of our choices are profoundly self-destructive. I will have something to say about that possibility in Chapter 3. But in a free society, Mill and Hayek nonetheless provide a good place to start.

THREE OBJECTIONS

It should be clear that the "as judged by themselves" criterion runs into three immediate objections.

First: Suppose that people are manipulated into having some belief or engaging in some action—for example, buying a product or supporting a candidate. To evaluate this concern, we need to define manipulation and specify what is wrong with it.[13] Let us stipulate, very briskly, that manipulation is a way of tricking people. Manipulators typically exploit people's ignorance or behavioral biases. They do not sufficiently engage people's capacities for reflection and deliberation. A manipulator might encourage people to purchase a used car by emphasizing how sleek it looks (and downplaying the fact that it is likely to break down), or to join a health club by showing photographs of healthy, beautiful people (and downplaying the fact that the club has terrible facilities).

The first problem with manipulation, thus defined, is that it does not treat people with respect. It is disrespectful of human agency. The second problem involves the risk to well-being. Because manipulators do not put people in a good position to make choices about what will actually promote their own interests and reflect their own values, they threaten to reduce people's welfare as well.

When people are manipulated, they are deprived of the (full) ability to make choices on their own, simply because they are not given a fair or adequate chance to weigh all relevant variables. To that extent, victims of manipulation are less free. Manipulation is a close cousin to coercion; it belongs in the same family. At the same time, manipulators often lack relevant knowledge—about the chooser's situation, tastes, and values. Lacking that knowledge, they nonetheless subvert the process by which good choosers make their own decisions about what is best for them.

Things are even worse if the manipulator is focused on his own interests rather than on those of choosers. Modern advertisers and modern politicians are often focused in just this way. It is in this sense that a self-interested manipulator can be said to be stealing from people—failing to respect their agency and moving their resources in the manipulator's preferred direction. Manipulators are thieves. If manipulation has occurred and if it is wrong, we would have an objection, even if people end up happy or satisfied after the fact.[14] To that extent, it makes sense to reject manipulation, even if the "as judged by themselves" standard is met.

Second: Suppose that people are nudged to accept some view or to engage in some act that runs into an independent moral objection. For example, people might be nudged to be racist or sexist. If the nudge works, they might be satisfied with their racism or sexism. The "as judged by themselves" criterion would be met. Even if so, the independent moral objection holds.[15] To that extent, the criterion is not sufficient.

Third: Consider the chilling last lines of George Orwell's *1984*: "He had won the victory over himself. He loved Big Brother."

These lines signal the final defeat of Orwell's hero, Winston Smith, who has been nudged by Orwell's villain, O'Brien, not only to *do* as the Party wishes but to *think* as the Party wishes—and to embrace his new thinking (almost erotically; actually, we can delete the "almost"). It is true that Smith has not merely been nudged; he has been manipulated and terrified and effectively coerced. But even if he had merely been nudged, an objection would remain. The reason is that Smith ends up in a state of effective slavery, even if or perhaps because he is content with that state. So much, you might say, for the "as judged by themselves" criterion.

Aldous Huxley's *Brave New World* is a different kind of dystopian novel, but Huxley makes the same point: "A really efficient totalitarian state would be one in which the all-powerful executive of political bosses and their army of managers control a population of slaves who do not have to be coerced, because they love their servitude."[16] Hence the plea of Huxley's hero, the Savage: "But I don't want comfort. I want God, I want poetry, I want real danger, I want freedom, I want goodness. I want sin."[17] Or consider this passage:[18]

"All right then," said the Savage defiantly, I'm claiming the right to be unhappy."

"Not to mention the right to grow old and ugly and impotent; the right to have syphilis and cancer; the right to have too little to eat, the right to be lousy; the right to live in constant apprehension of what may happen tomorrow; the right to catch typhoid; the right to be tortured by unspeakable pains of every kind."

There was a long silence.

"I claim them all," said the Savage at last.

What must be said here is that even if people believe that they are better off, and even if the "as judged by themselves" criterion is met, they might be in a state of unfreedom, because they might not be experiencing a sufficiently human life, in which they are able to experience agency and autonomy. That is a fundamental point. But it should not be taken as an objection to most real-world nudging, at least in democratic societies, where the goal is often to promote navigability and to increase people's capacity for agency and autonomy (consider disclosure of information), and when efforts to make life easier hardly create servitude (consider automatic enrollment in pension plans).

PUZZLES

In this light, we might conclude that while it is (almost always) necessary to meet the "as judged by themselves" criterion, meeting that criterion is not (always) sufficient. At least this is so if we care about freedom. The conclusion is generally right. And beyond these qualifications, it is certainly reasonable to wonder about potential ambiguities in that criterion. Most important:

- Should the focus be on choosers' judgments before the nudge, or instead after? What if the nudge alters people's preferences, so that they like the outcome produced by the nudge, when they would not have sought that outcome in advance? What if preferences are constructed by the relevant choice architecture?

- What if people's before-the-fact judgments are wrong, in the sense that a nudge would improve their well-being, even though they do not think that it will?

- Do we want to ask about choosers' actual, potentially uninformed or behaviorally biased judgments, or are we entitled to ask what choosers would think if they had all relevant information and were unaffected by relevant biases?

To make progress on questions of this kind, three categories of cases should be distinguished:

1. Those in which choosers have clear antecedent preferences, and nudges help them to satisfy those preferences.

2. Those in which choosers face a self-control problem, and nudges help them to overcome that problem.

3. Those in which choosers would be content with the outcomes produced by two or more nudges, or in which after-the-fact preferences are a product of or constructed by nudges, so that the "as judged by themselves" criterion leaves choice architects with several options, without specifying which one to choose.

Cases that fall in category (1) plainly satisfy the "as judged by themselves" criterion—and there are many such cases. They involve navigability. From the standpoint of the "as judged by themselves" criterion, cases that fall in category (2)—reminiscent of *Genesis* and *Possession*—are also unobjectionable, indeed they can be seen to involve navigability and as a subset of category (1). They too are plentiful, but they have their own complexities. Cases that fall in category (3) create special challenges, which may lead us to make direct inquiries into people's well-being or to explore what informed, active choosers typically select.

CHAPTER 2
NAVIGABILITY

For many years, the United States relied on the "Food Pyramid" as its central icon to promote healthy eating. Created by the Department of Agriculture, the Food Pyramid was one of the most visited websites in the entire U.S. government. Countless parents and children used it.

Here's what it looked like:

The Pyramid was long criticized as hopelessly uninformative. The reason is that it does not provide people with any kind of clear path with respect to healthy diets. A shoeless person appears to be climbing to the top of a pyramid. But why? The pyramid is organized by five stripes. (Or is it seven?) What do they connote? At the bottom, you can see a lot of different foods. But it's a mess. Some of the foods appear to fall in several categories. Are some grains vegetables?

People are unlikely to change their behavior if they do not know what to do. A lot of people are interested in healthy eating, but they are unaware of the concrete steps that they should take. The Food Pyramid did not much help.

A number of years ago, the Department of Agriculture consulted with a wide range of experts, with backgrounds in both nutrition and communication, to explore what kind of icon might be better. In the end, the Department replaced the Pyramid with a new, simpler icon, consisting of a plate with clear markings for fruits, vegetables, grains, and protein. Here it is:

The plate is designed to give clear, simple guidance—to be a kind of map. Of course, it doesn't require anyone to do anything. But it makes it clear that if half your plate is fruits and vegetables, you'll be doing well, and if the rest of the plate is divided between rice and meat (or some other protein), you're likely to be having a healthy meal.

At the same time, the plate is accompanied by straightforward verbal tips, available on choosemyplate.gov, giving people information about what they might do if they want to make good nutritional choices. The tips change periodically but here are recent examples:

- make half your plate fruits and vegetables
- drink water instead of sugary drinks
- switch to fat-free or low-fat (1%) milk
- choose unsalted nuts and seeds to keep sodium intake low

These statements have the key advantage of avoiding vagueness and ambiguity. The tips are clear and "actionable." Of course we might be able to do better than the Food Plate, and some other tips might be better. But for employers, parents, public interest organizations, advertisers, and public officials, "Plate, not Pyramid" is a terrific organizing principle: Identify the favored path.

GETTING THERE

There's an old story about a tourist who had been in New York City for about a week, and who had a sense of how New Yorkers responded to his questions. One day he went up to a New Yorker and asked, "Can you tell me how to get to the Empire State Building—or should I just go to hell?"

Okay, it's a joke, not a story, but it says something important about the human condition. Often we need directions, and it's not exactly fun to ask. If we do, the answer might be, "Go to hell." If no human being is available to give that answer or a more helpful one, we might find that the design is not operating in our favor. It is telling us to go to hell.

Imagine that you are in an airport in an unfamiliar city, that you are running late, and that you need to find your gate in a hurry. You are making a mad dash. Suppose that the signs are in a foreign language and that you cannot figure out where you need to go. Or suppose that in order to enroll your child in school, you are asked to fill out certain forms online. Suppose that the forms are massively confusing. Some of the links do not work; you cannot figure out how to do what is required. Or suppose that you are staying in a hotel on a business trip, and you enter a badly needed shower, only to find that it contains a series of knobs in puzzling places. You cannot tell how to turn it on or to get the temperature you like. Or suppose that your child seems to be suffering from a mental health problem; it might be anxiety or depression, or it might be something else. You might not know, and might not know how to get help. If you call the local doctor, you might not get helpful guidance, or you might not understand what you're told.

In one or another form, these are common problems. The stakes can be small or they can be large. In trivial cases, you lose time, and you get frustrated. In less trivial cases, something that really matters must be put on hold. In serious cases, you might be unable to solve a problem of defining importance to your life.

All of these examples illustrate the point that I mean to press: Obstacles to navigability decrease freedom, even if people retain freedom of choice. As the GPS device and Food Plate examples suggest, many nudges, and many forms of choice architecture, have the goal of increasing navigability—of making it easier for people to get to their preferred destination. Life can be simple or hard to navigate, and helpful choice architecture promotes simple navigation.

We can understand the problem of navigability in several different ways. A celebrated mathematician, John Dee, offered a definition in 1570: "The Arte of Navigation, demonstrateth how, by the shortest good way, by the aptest Direction, & in the shortest time, a sufficient Ship, between any two places . . . assigned; may be conducted."[1] For present purposes, that definition is essentially perfect.

Dee's words can be understood to point to three different problems. First, people might not know, or might have difficulty seeing or finding, the right or best path. Second, people might see or be able to find the right path, or in some sense know it in theory, but might have difficulty finding the motivation to get on it. Third, people might face a wide range of difficult choices, which might make it hard for them to focus on getting on the right path. Like Dee's, my emphasis in this chapter is on the first understanding. I will have something to say about the second and the third in the next chapter.

If we care about freedom, making the world more navigable might not seem like the most ambitious imaginable idea, but it has immense importance. Many of the problems we face stem from insufficient navigability. For poor people, that is indeed a pervasive problem. Consider these words from the economist Esther Duflo:[2]

We tend to be patronizing about the poor in a very specific sense, which is that we tend to think, "Why don't they take more responsibility for their lives?" And what we are forgetting is that the richer you are the less responsibility you need to take for your own life because everything is taken care for you. And the poorer you are the more you have

to be responsible for everything about your
life. . . . [S]top berating people for not being
responsible and start to think of ways instead
of providing the poor with the luxury that we
all have, which is that a lot of decisions are
taken for us. If we do nothing, we are on the
right track. For most of the poor, if they do
nothing, they are on the wrong track.

In my terms, the problem is that they have
to *find* the right track—to identify the right
doctor, to get a good lawyer, to find the right
job, to get help in taking care of children. With
respect to freedom, that is a serious problem.
All over the world, efforts to increase navigability can make all the difference. Good cities are easily navigated; so are good airports;
so are good websites. A GPS device respects
people's ends; it does not quarrel with their
judgment about their preferred destination.

But it helps them get where they want to go. It does not make them think. Many nudges, having nothing to with literal navigation, can be understood in similar terms (above all default rules, which promote good outcomes even if people do nothing). Other nudges require some thinking—consider information, reminders, and warnings—but they do not impose serious burdens on those whom they are designed to help, and they also increase navigability.

The stakes are high. In recent years, researchers have devoted a great deal of attention to the subject of happiness, which we may take, for present purposes, as a surrogate for well-being. In many nations, unhappiness is a product of mental illness. In many others, it is a product of unemployment. Increases in navigability can enable those who suffer from mental illness to get some help. Increases in navigability can help people to find employment. With such approaches, freedom is hardly compromised. On the contrary, it is increased. And with such approaches, well-being is increased as well.

WHERE DO YOU WANT TO GO?

In the simplest cases, people have a clear sense of their preferred destination, and it is concrete. They want to find the local gas station. They are looking for a good dentist near their home. They want to attend a college in a particular city.

In other cases, their destination is more abstract and a bit vague. They want to have a good job. They want to go to a good college. They want to find a spouse. In still other cases, people have a sense of their preferred destination, but it operates at a very high level of abstraction. They want to find peace. They want to be loved. They want their lives to be good. In some of these cases, the destination is so abstract that it is fair to doubt whether they really know where they want to go. In some situations, the idea of navigability seems inadequate, just because choosers cannot specify where they want to end up.

In short, there is a continuum from the most concrete to the most abstract destinations, and in some cases, people cannot readily specify their preferred destination at all. The easiest situations involve concrete destinations, so that the chooser is seeking a way "between any two places . . . assigned." My emphasis here is on concrete destinations and easy cases. But in the hardest situations, the choice architect, purporting to help solve a navigability problem, might actually be pointing the chooser toward a destination that the chooser has not identified. Those situations are harder because the choice architect cannot say, "I am respecting your ends and simply helping you to find a way

to get there." But so long as the choice architect can point to *something* that the chooser
embraces—health, longevity, peace—and so
long as the chooser retains freedom of choice
and judges the destination to be a good one, the
difficulty is reduced.

NAVIGABILITY AND SLUDGE

Consider three examples:

1. Luke has heart disease, and he needs to take
   various medications. He wants to do so, but
   he is sometimes forgetful. His doctor sends
   him periodic text messages. As a result, he
   takes the medications. He is very glad to receive those messages.
2. Meredith has a mild weight problem. She is
   aware of that fact, and while she does not
   suffer from serious issues of self-control, and

does not want to stop eating the foods that she enjoys, she does seek to lose weight. Because of a new law, many restaurants in her city have clear calorie labels, informing her of the caloric content of various options. As a result, she sometimes chooses low-calorie offerings—which she would not do if she were not informed. She is losing weight. She is very glad to see those calorie labels.

3. Rita teaches at a school, which has long offered its employees the option to sign up for a retirement plan. Rita believes that signing up would be a terrific idea, but she has not gotten around to it. She is somewhat embarrassed about that. Last year, the school switched to an automatic enrollment plan, by which employees are defaulted into the school's plan. They are allowed to opt out, but Rita does not. She is very glad that she has been automatically enrolled in the plan.

In all of these cases, the relevant intervention increases navigability. Nor is there is anything unfamiliar about such cases. On the contrary, they capture a great deal of the real-world terrain of nudging, both by governments and by the private sector. A well-studied and instructive example involves control of asthma. Patients and their families know that they want to reduce the risk of serious health problems, but they might not know how to do that, and they have to work together with their doctor to find a good path.[3] In countless cases, choosers have a goal, or an assortment of goals, and the relevant choice architecture makes it easier for them to achieve it or them. Insofar as we understand the "as judged by themselves" criterion by reference to people's antecedent preferences, that criterion is met.

Note that it would be easy to design variations on these cases in which nudges *failed* that criterion, because they would make people worse off by their own lights. Richard Thaler uses the term "sludge" for practices that reduce navigability. Unfortunately and sometimes tragically, sludge is everywhere.[4] Sludge reduces freedom, in the sense that it makes it harder for people to get where they want to go. We might go further: In many nations, sludge is a principal obstacle to freedom.

As I have described them, the cases of Luke, Meredith, and Rita are relatively simple, because the nudge really does help them to arrive at their preferred destination. But in some cases, people have clear antecedent preferences, and the nudge is inconsistent with those preferences—but as a result of the nudge, their preferences are changed. For example:

Jonathan likes talking on his cell phone while driving. He talks to friends on his commute to work, and he does business as well. As a result of a set of vivid warnings, he has stopped. He is glad. He cannot imagine why anyone would talk on a cell phone while driving. In his view, that is too dangerous.

After the nudge, Jonathan believes himself to be better off—no less than Luke, Meredith, and Rita. But Jonathan's case raises a question. The "as judged by themselves" criterion seems to ask how people think and feel *after the nudge.* Do they believe themselves to be better off? But we might wonder whether that is the right question when people think and feel, before the nudge, that all is well, and that a nudge is not necessary or desirable. I will turn to that question in due course. My main point is that as originally given, the cases of Luke, Elizabeth, and Rita are straightforward. Such cases are common.

I hope that I have said enough to show that problems of navigability are pervasive in human life, and that they present a serious obstacle to freedom. It is perfectly fine to insist that in general, people should be free to choose. That is true and important. But even when people are free to choose, they may not know how to get to their preferred destination. Improvements in navigability are not a modest achievement. They can make all the difference.

CHAPTER 3
SELF-CONTROL

As a young man, Saint Augustine prayed, "Lord, make me chaste—but not yet." The prayer expresses a free choice on behalf of chastity, alongside a free choice in favor of sexual activity (for now). Or consider these words from Christabel LaMotte in Byatt's *Possession*: "I cannot let you burn me up, nor can I resist you. No mere human can stand in a fire and not be consumed."

Here is a dilemma of freedom. Sometimes we refuse to be burned up (the refusal is a choice), and sometimes we are unable to resist. Is that a choice? Sometimes. LaMotte stood in a fire and was consumed; that is how she exercised her freedom.

Philosophers, economists, psychologists, lawyers, and others have long been concerned with a variety of problems that go under the general rubric of "self-control." Philosophers speak of weakness of will, which refers to susceptibility to temptation—too much food, too much drink, too much sex, too little concern for the future. Many people emphasize impatience. Franz Kafka, focusing on Genesis, proclaimed, "There are two main human sins from which all the others derive: impatience and indolence. It was because of impatience that they were expelled from Paradise; it is because of indolence that they do not return. Yet perhaps there is only one major sin: impatience. Because of impatience they were expelled, because of impatience they do not return."[1]

Some social scientists like to describe addiction as a "disorder of choice," capturing both personal agency and the distortions involved.[2]

A patient of Benjamin Rush, sometimes described as the father of American psychiatry, was eloquent about that particular disorder and about self-control problems in general: "Were a keg of rum in one corner of the room, and were cannon constantly discharging balls between me and it, I could not refrain from passing before that cannon, in order to get at the rum."[3]

Economists and psychologists speak of present bias and unrealistic optimism, which may lead people to injure their long-term selves. They also refer to two families of cognitive operations of the human mind: System 1 and System 2.[4] System 1 is the fast, intuitive, automatic system (focused on today and tomorrow), and System 2 is the slower, more reflective, deliberative system (capable of taking the long view).

A small story: I have a nine-year-old son, named Declan, who loves toys. Whenever we pass a toy store, he wants to stop and get something. A few years ago, I told him about the difference between the two systems, and I explained that while his System 1 wants toys, his System 2 is well aware that he has plenty of toys and has no need for more. (Doesn't every good father explain that?) For a while, he understood the point, and it seemed to help. But after a month, he asked me, "Daddy, do I even *have* a System 2?" I didn't have the presence of mind to answer that the very question showed that he did.

Self-control problems raise conceptual, empirical, and normative challenges. They also create many puzzles about freedom. An addiction is an extreme version of a self-control problem, and the word "addiction" derives from one of the Latin words for slave; it connotes a kind of bondage or servitude. Outside of the context of addictions, a pervasive question is whether those who indulge themselves, today or this month, suffer from a self-control problem, or instead have a fully rational mantra: "Enjoy life now. This is not a rehearsal." Another question is whether purported solutions to self-control problems will make the situation better rather than worse. Some cures can be worse than the disease.

Consider these haunting, ambivalent words from LaMotte, writing to her dying, married lover, Randolph Ash: "I would rather have lived alone, so, if you would have the truth. But since that might not be—and is granted to almost none—I thank God for you—if there *must* be a Dragon—that He was You—."[5] (The structure of the sentence belies her claim that she "would rather have lived alone." Her System 1 knew better.) Readers of *Genesis* have long pondered whether the choices of Adam and Eve in the Garden of Eden reflected a fatal inability to resist temptation (the conventional view) or something very different, such as an exercise of autonomy or an honorable thirst for knowledge (and in an important sense freedom). Was the serpent only or altogether a villain? Was he a villain at all? Might he have been a hero? Was he doing God's work? The conventional view has triumphed in most circles, but the appeal of the alternative view helps account for the complexity and the enduring power of *Genesis*.

Notwithstanding these debates and La-Motte's ambivalence, there is no question that many people agree, before and after the fact, that interventions can help them overcome self-control problems, even if they preserve freedom of choice. We should be familiar with relatively simple cases in which people have a preference at Time 1; make certain choices at Time 2; and regret those choices at Time 3. Perhaps an intervention will eliminate the conflict.

Perhaps an intervention, or a nudge, will increase freedom. For example:

1. *Ted smokes cigarettes. He wishes that he had never started, but he has been unable to quit. He regrets his habit. His government recently imposed a new requirement, which is that cigarette packages must be accompanied with graphic images, showing people with serious health problems, including lung cancer. Ted is deeply affected by those images; he cannot bear to see them. He quits, and he is glad.*

2. *Joan is a student at a large university. She drinks a lot of alcohol. She enjoys it, but not that much, and she is worried that her drinking is impairing her performance and her health. She says that she would like to scale back, but for reasons that she does not entirely understand, she has found it difficult to do so. Her university recently embarked on*

an educational campaign to reduce drinking on campus, in which it (accurately) notes that four out of five students drink only twice a month or less. Informed of the social norm, Joan finally resolves to cut back her drinking. She does, and she is glad.

3. Kendra texts while driving. She has known that is not a good idea, and she vowed to stop. But she didn't. Her state banned texting while driving; it is now a crime. She no longer texts while driving. She is glad.

In these cases, the chooser suffers from a self-control problem and is fully aware of that fact. Ted, Joan, and Kendra can be seen as both planners, with second-order preferences, and doers, with first-order preferences. In the cases of Ted and Joan, a nudge helps to strengthen the hand of the planner. In the case of Kendra, a legal prohibition has the same effect.

The point suggests a more general one, which is that some legal bans may not only promote people's well-being (by preventing deaths and injuries) but in a sense increase their freedom as well. At least this is so when they help people to achieve an outcome that they favor but cannot bring about on their own. Like Ulysses seeking to resist the Sirens, people may want some kind of precommitment strategy, even though, or because, it constrains their own actions.

I am emphasizing a more modest point here: Ted and Joan welcome the relevant nudges, and do so before the fact and after the fact. The "as judged by themselves" criterion is met. In an important respect, Ted, Joan, and Kendra are freer once their self-control problem has been solved.

Cases that involve serious addictions have important wrinkles, but for my purposes, they are analogous. Addicts are especially likely to show present bias (sometimes described as "delay discounting").[6] Many alcoholics, smokers, and drug addicts want to quit, but they feel that they cannot. They think that their freedom has been compromised. As Alcoholics Anonymous puts it, "[M]ost alcoholics . . . have lost the power of choice in drink. Our so-called will power becomes practically non-existent." Consider the words of the actor Russell Brand: "The mentality and behavior of drug addicts and alcoholics is wholly irrational until you understand that they are completely powerless over their addiction and unless they have structured help they have no hope."[7] The singer Stevie Nicks put it this way: "I used to carry a gram of cocaine in my boot, and it was the first thing I thought of when I woke up in the morning and the last thing I thought of when I went to bed."[8] A long-time heroin addict captured the simultaneous feeling of bondage and choice: "My marriage would fall apart, I'd lose the house, and knowing all these things I was doing, I still chose heroin. I still chose heroin."[9]

For addicts, the question is how to quit. Many addicts do not know.[10] A nudge might be the answer.[11] Addiction has been described as a "blindfold," with explicit reference to the problem of navigability:[12]

A blindfolded man often stumbles where others can tread safely. He can't see what lies before him; he is unaware of the dangers he may be facing; he is ignorant of the best way to proceed. . . . The best way of leading a blindfolded man out of difficulty is by guiding him gently, encouraging him not to be scared, and helping him to navigate when he's not sure which way to go. . . . Addicts are essentially blindfolded individuals and are often aware of how blind they are.

The analogy holds for many self-control problems. But addiction is an extreme case, and some apparent self-control problems are not nearly as simple as they seem. Recall the basic structure: people have a preference at Time 1; they make certain choices at Time 2; they regret those choices at Time 3. In such cases, we should underline the fact that when outsiders, including choice architects, contend that choosers suffer from a self-control problem, they ought to be humble. Doesn't Time 2 have a claim? Mightn't it be the most important time of all? The questions suggest that outsiders face an epistemic problem. They are like social planners, trying to intervene in a market, and they might not know what they do not know.[13]

Choosers might not, in fact, be adversely affected by present bias or inertia; they might love what they are doing, even if it harms their future self, and they might be making a rational, or rational enough, trade-off between now and later. Consider a delicious meal, a wild night, two weeks off, an incautious love affair. Life is not a rehearsal, and planners need to do. What they do is also an exercise of freedom. What doers do might be one of the most significant and best experiences of their lives—even if they would have chosen otherwise in advance and perhaps even if they regret it afterwards.

For that reason, we need to offer a cautionary note, signaled by LaMotte's words: Her System 1 did not regret what happened, and sometimes, System 1 rules the roost. And perhaps her System 2 would agree, on reflection. (I think it did.) We could complicate the cases of Ted and Joan by noting the possibility that at the time of choice (whether to smoke, whether to drink), both of them might see that the benefits of indulging are actually very great. Sure, both of them wish that they had refrained at Time 1, and showed regret at Time 3. But at Time 2, both choosers knew something important; and perhaps they were not wrong at that time. Under these assumptions, it is possible that in terms of well-being, Ted and Joan are worse off if we give authority to their pre-choice and post-choice selves. Time 2 does have its claims.

It is nonetheless true that in important cases, self-control problems are serious and real, and choosers will acknowledge that fact. For both Ted and Joan, the argument I have just sketched seems far-fetched. In a sense, solutions to self-control problems require their own GPS devices and so involve navigability. Appropriate interventions lead people where they want to go (at least on reflection). They promote freedom. For choosers who face self-control problems, the underlying challenge is qualitatively distinctive—it is not a simple problem of insufficient knowledge—and they recognize that fact.

WHAT DO PEOPLE THINK?

In the cases I am exploring, the "as judged by themselves" criterion is met. But do people know that they face self-control problems? That is an empirical question, of course, and my own preliminary research suggests that the answer is "yes." On Amazon's Mechanical Turk (a platform that allows online surveys of large numbers of people), I asked about 200 people this question:

Many people believe that they have an issue, whether large or small, of self-control. They may eat too much, they may smoke, they may drink too much, they may not save enough money. Do you believe that you have any issue of self-control?

No less than 70 percent said that they did (55 percent said "somewhat agree," while 15 percent said "strongly agree"). Only 22 percent disagreed. Eight percent were neutral.

This is a preliminary test, of course, and the answers are only suggestive. The larger point is that whatever majorities say, the cases of Ted and Mary capture a lot of the territory of human life, as reflected in the immense popularity of programs designed to help people to combat addiction to tobacco and alcohol. We should agree that nudges that do the work of such programs, or that are used in such programs, are likely to satisfy the "as judged by themselves" criterion. They increase navigability and they promote freedom.

HARDER CASES

In many situations, the problem is much more complicated, and so is the analysis of freedom.[14] We can imagine cases in which an agent is consistent; he wants to have a drink at Time 1, he does so at Time 2, and he is happy that he did so at Time 3. The cases of Ted and Mary involve inconsistency in a special sense: An agent wants to abstain at Time 1, he smokes or drinks at Time 2, and he regrets his choice at Time 3. But we could imagine other combinations.

Suppose, for example, that the agent has no particular view at Time 1 (maybe he has not thought about the issue), but makes a decision at Time 2 that he regrets at Time 3. Consider these cases:

1. *John is at a dinner celebration. The food is terrific. He eats a lot of it. He has a wonderful time. The next day, he steps on the scale, and he finds*

that he has gained two pounds. He wishes that he had not eaten so much. He feels terrible.

2. Edith is at a work-related conference for a week. She is happily married. She meets a married man named Charles, and there is an immediate attraction. They have a brief, steamy, wonderful romance. When she comes home, she feels terrible about it. She does not tell her husband, but the memory haunts her; she wishes the romance had never happened.

Of course the two cases are different. John's case is relatively trivial; Edith's does not appear to be. But they have the same structure. Both John and Edith succumbed to temptation, and at the time, they were delighted to do so. They chose freely. Afterwards, they felt regret, and concluded that they made a mistake. If John or Edith had been in the position of planner at Time 1—say, a week before—they might well have wanted some kind of commitment device, or nudge, to prevent the mistake from happening. It is tempting to think that the planner has a kind of authority, or authenticity, and that if the planner is put together with the regretter (as we might call him), the cases are not so hard after all.

That conclusion is probably right, but as I have signaled, it might be too simple. Why does John or Edith deserve authority at Time 1 or Time 3, rather than Time 2? What makes either of their views authoritative or authentic, rather than the choice at Time 2? What makes the planner so special, or the regretter? To be sure, both John and Edith might have had less than complete knowledge at the time of choice; in all probability, they did not fully or adequately appreciate the consequences of their choices. They were exporting costs to their future selves. They might have ignored or undervalued those costs. That is important; it suggests a good reason to deny authority, in some cases, to the chooser at the time of choice. But at Time 1 or Time 3, there might well be incomplete knowledge as well, or at least incomplete appreciation of the situation at Time 2.

Once again: At Time 1, at least, the planner might be like a social planner, facing a serious epistemic deficit. The same might be true of the regretter, who does not give sufficient weight to the experience at Time 2. After the fact, the regretter might be undervaluing the importance of that experience. The experiencing self might have too little regard for the remembering self, but the converse is also true. It is not clear that either deserves priority. To know, we might have to make some moral judgments, or offer some account of how to aggregate well-being over time. A terrific weekend is most unlikely to justify years of regret or distress.

We could further complicate matters by assuming that at Time 1, John and Edith would have chosen a commitment device, stopping them from doing what they did—but that at Time 3, after the conduct has occurred, both of them are glad, on balance, that they did not. As in:

> *Edith is at a work-related conference for a week. She is happily married. She meets a man named Charles, and there is an immediate attraction. They have a steamy, wonderful romance. When she comes home, she feels both thrilled and terrible about it. She does not tell her husband, and the memory haunts her; but she is glad that the romance happened. She hopes that the romance will continue—not often, but perhaps once a year, and for many years.*

Consider a different problem, in which the agent would probably not have chosen a commitment device, but with overlapping features:

Eric is a corporate lawyer. He likes his life; he makes plenty of money, and he feels good, or good enough, about what he does. The idea of doing something different does not appeal to him. On a vacation, he meets Janet, a public interest lawyer who works on environmental cases. After a lunch, he decides that he wants to change his career. He wants to work on causes that he cares about. He quits his job. He is glad that he did.

In cases like those of Edith and Eric, it is not possible to resolve the question by asking what the chooser actually wants. The chooser actually wants different things at different times. Moreover, the "as judged by themselves"

standard has an ambiguity: As judged by themselves, *when*? I have suggested that the standard
calls for an inquiry into what the choose thinks
after the fact. But if the chooser has one view in
January and another in June, it is not clear that
June deserves authority.

In my view, there is no alternative to resort-
ing to some kind of external standard, involv-
ing a judgment about what makes the chooser's
life better, all things considered. That judgment
might require moral evaluations of options
and outcomes. It might require some kind of
aggregate judgment about people's personal
well-being. In many cases in which people think
differently at Time 1, Time 2, and Time 3, we
have to ask: "What is the effect of honoring one
or another thought on the person's well-being
over time?" In the case of Edith, for example,
her decision at Time 2 might (on plausible assumptions) effectively ruin her life, in which

case it would be hard to say that that decision was right. But (putting moral issues to one side) we could also imagine that her decision at Time 2 was one of the best, and most precious, that she ever made. Valuing freedom of choice does not tell us what we need to know.

That brings us directly to our next topic.

CHAPTER 4

HAPPY EITHER WAY

In many cases, we know what we want, and the question is how to get it. That was my focus in Chapter 2. In some cases, we are divided. There is a difference between what we want to want before the time of choice, what we want at the time of choice, and what we want to have wanted after the time of choice. That was my focus in Chapter 3.

But in some cases, it is not clear if we have antecedent preferences at all. Perhaps we do not. We might have no idea what we want. We might lack important information, and if we have it, we still might not know what we want. In other cases, our after-the-fact preferences are an artifact of, or constructed by, the nudge. Sometimes these two factors are combined (as savvy marketers are well-aware). We are speaking here of "endogenous preferences," and in particular of *preferences that are endogenous to, or a product of, the relevant choice architecture*. In such cases, how should we think about freedom of choice? And how ought the "as judged by themselves" criterion to be understood and applied?

A clarification: I am not making or engaging large claims about the social construction of preferences, values, or beliefs, or exploring either philosophical or sociological arguments about the role of social norms. The point is more specific and even mundane: People's preferences and values, and not merely their actions, can be a product of some nudge, such a default rule, and *they may end up happy and satisfied however they are nudged*. With some default settings on your cell phone, you might think, "great, that makes perfect sense," and stick with them; if the settings were otherwise, you might think the same thing. Exercising your freedom of choice, you decide to stay with the status quo, whatever it is. That raises some dilemmas for those who are deciding what the status quo should be.

Let us start with some fairly mundane cases:

1. *George cares about the environment, but he also cares about money. He currently receives his electricity from coal; he knows that coal is not exactly good for the environment, but it is cheap, and he does not bother to switch to wind, which would be slightly more expensive. He is quite content with the current situation. Last month, his government imposed an automatic enrollment rule on electricity providers: People will receive energy from wind, and pay a slight premium, unless they choose to switch. George does not bother to switch. He says that*

he likes the current situation of automatic enrollment. He approves of the policy and he approves of his own enrollment.

2. Diane is automatically enrolled in a Bronze Health Care Plan—it is less expensive than Silver and Gold, but it is also less comprehensive in its coverage, and it has a higher deductible. Diane prefers Bronze and has no interest in switching. In a parallel world (a lot like ours, but not quite identical), Diane is automatically enrolled in a Gold Health Care Plan—it is more expensive than Silver and Bronze, but it is also more comprehensive in its coverage, and it has a lower deductible. In that parallel world, Diane prefers Gold and has no interest in switching.

3. Thomas has a serious illness. The question is whether he should have an operation, which carries with it with potential benefits and potential risks. Reading about the operation

online, Thomas is not sure whether he should go ahead with it. Thomas's doctor advises him to have the operation, emphasizing how much he has to lose if he does not. He decides to follow the advice. In a parallel world (a lot like ours, but not quite identical), Thomas's doctor advises him not to have the operation, emphasizing how much he has to lose if he does. He decides to follow the advice.

I have noted that science fiction writers like to speak of "parallel worlds," showing that with a little twist or a small alteration, our families, our lives, our cities, our nations, our entire world might be very different. (Again from *Possession*, after a fateful, heartbreaking encounter: "There are things that happen and leave no discernible trace, are not spoken or written of, though it would be very wrong to say that subsequent events go on indifferently, all the same, as though such things had never been."[1]) Parallel worlds are intriguing for many reasons, and the very idea is (I think) deep, because it highlights the omnipresence and the power of contingency. One such reason is that we—you and I—might have been, or be, quite happy in multiple other worlds, even if we are quite happy in our own. Our choices might be different in such worlds, even if they are free in every one of them. For the "as judged by themselves" criterion, that is a serious challenge. It suggests that the criterion does not produce unique solutions.

History is only run once, but nudges can be taken to create parallel worlds. In the latter two cases, Diane and Thomas appear to lack an antecedent preference; what they prefer is an artifact of the default rule (in the case of Diane) or the framing (in the case of Thomas). George's case is different. He *does* have an antecedent preference. We might think that in cases like his, nudges are illegitimate and even analogous to the case of Winston in *1984*. Perhaps we should establish a clear rule: *If a nudge is inconsistent with a chooser's current preferences, it should not be adopted.*

But why? After all, a chooser can reject the nudge and go his own way, if that is what he wants to do. And if a chooser does not reject the nudge and ends up happy or satisfied with the situation in which he finds himself, post-nudge, then there would seem to be no objection, at least on welfare grounds. True, we could raise an autonomy concern and say that if people are happy with their situation, they should not be nudged away from it. But it is hard, I think, to defend that idea so long as people retain freedom of choice and in the end are satisfied ("as judged by themselves"). In *1984*, Winston's situation is abhorrent because he has been terrorized (and coerced as well as nudged) into a state of unfreedom. The same can hardly be said of George.

As the three cases suggest, I am focusing on a specific problem: *What people like is a product of the nudge.* Their preference is constructed by it. After being nudged, they will be happy and possibly grateful.

There are many possible reasons. One might be the power of suggestion: The nudge might come with some kind of informational signal ("the Bronze Plan is better!"), and people might hear that signal. Another reason might be learning: People might see that the situation is good, or good enough, and might therefore be content with it (whatever it is). Yet another reason might be "status quo bias": People tend to stick with, or prefer, the status quo, whatever it is.[2] A related reason might be reduction of cognitive dissonance: People might reduce dissonance in a way that makes them satisfied with the new status quo, whatever it is. If so, it is hard to see the "as judged by themselves" criterion as sufficient, because by hypothesis, people are satisfied only because dissatisfaction is unpleasant or unbearable, and because they would be satisfied either way.

We have also seen that even if people have an antecedent preference or value, the nudge might change it, so that they will be happy and possibly grateful after the fact, even if they did not want to be nudged in advance. The most extreme cases involve "Big Decisions"[3] or "transformative experiences,"[4] in which people's identity, and their preferences and values, are at stake. After they make certain decisions, or are nudged to make them, what they care about, and who they most deeply are, are different from what they were before. People might, for example, decide to have a romance, to get married, to have children, to change occupations, to change cities. Some of these decisions turn out to be defining. (From *Possession*: "This is where I have always been coming to. Since my time began. And when I go away from here, this will be the midpoint, to which everything ran, before, and *from* which everything will run. But now, my love, we are *now*, and those other times are running elsewhere."[5])

In the philosophical literature, transformative experiences are often assessed from the first-person perspective: How should you or I choose between the status quo and undergoing some kind of transformation? The question I am posing here is different: How should we evaluate transformative nudges?

In extreme and mundane cases, application of the "as judged by themselves" criterion is much less simple whenever people's preferences are an artifact of nudging. The question of freedom also becomes more vexing. Choice architects cannot contend that they are increasing navigability or merely vindicating choosers' antecedent preferences. If we look after the fact, people do think that they are better off, and in that sense the criterion is met. For use of the "as judged by themselves" criterion, the challenge is that *however Diane and Thomas are nudged, they will agree that they are better off*. In my view, there is no escaping an inquiry into well-being in choosing between the two worlds in the cases of Diane and Thomas. We need to ask what kind of approach makes people's lives go better.[6]

NARROWING OPTIONS

I will get to that question in due course. Let us note preliminarily that the "as judged by themselves" criterion remains relevant in the sense that it constrains what choice architects can do, even if it does not specify a unique outcome (as it does in simple cases of navigability, or other cases in which people have clear antecedent preferences and in which the nudge does not alter them).

Recall that it is reasonable to think that some choosers have antecedent preferences, but that because of a lack of information or a behavioral bias, their free choices will not satisfy them. (See the cases of Luke, Meredith, and Rita.) It is also imaginable that some forms of choice architecture will affect people who do have information or who lack such biases; an error-free cafeteria visitor might grab the first item she sees, because she is busy, and because it is not worth it to her to decide which item to choose. Consider this case:

Georgia enjoys her employer's cafeteria. She tends to eat high-calorie meals, but she knows that, and she likes them a lot. Her employer recently redesigned the cafeteria so that salads and fruits are the most visible and accessible. She now chooses salad and fruit, and she likes them a lot.

By stipulation, Georgia suffers from no behavioral bias, but she is affected by the nudge. But in many (standard) cases, behaviorally biased or uninformed choosers will be affected by a nudge, and less biased and highly informed choosers will not; a developing literature explores how to proceed in such cases, with careful reference to what seems to me a version of the "as judged by themselves" criterion.[7]

In Georgia's case, and all those like it, the criterion does not leave choice architects at sea. If she did not like the salad, the criterion would be violated. From the normative standpoint, it may not be entirely comforting to say that nudges satisfy the "as judged by themselves" criterion if choice architects succeed in altering the preferences of those whom they are targeting. (Is that a road to serfdom? Recall the chilling last lines of George Orwell's *1984*: "He had won the victory over himself. He loved Big Brother.") But insofar as we are concerned with people's well-being, it is a highly relevant question whether choosers believe, ex post, that the nudge has produced an outcome of which they approve.

TWO APPROACHES

Now let us engage the largest questions. If people would be happy, after the fact, with the outcome produced by two or more interventions, then which interventions ought choice architects to select? We have seen that the "as judged by themselves" criterion is indeterminate. In these circumstances, it is possible to imagine two approaches. Recall that we are operating within a commitment to freedom of choice. Whatever approach we take, we are allowing people to go their own way if that is what they want. The challenge is that what they want is a product of the approach we take.

Follow the right choosers

The first approach, elaborated by Stanford law professor Jacob Goldin, would be to ask about the actual choices of people who are (a) informed and (b) unaffected by the nudge.[8] On this approach, choice architects would attempt to follow those choices. They would not make decisions on their own. They would figure out what certain people—the most reliable choosers—actually do, and they would then design the choice architecture so that everyone is nudged to do that. We can associate this approach with John Stuart Mill's understanding of freedom, emphasizing his commitment to respecting people's choices about what would promote their well-being. The basic idea is that choice architects, respectful of freedom of choice, should try to identify the choices that informed people consistently make.

Consider this possibility:

In a large population of choosers, a subset of people chooses a particular health care plan, no matter how they are nudged. They are well-informed. In terms of what they care about, they are not different, in any relevant respect, from people who are highly susceptible to nudges, and who are happy, after the fact, whether or not they are nudged. The well-informed people consistently choose a particular plan, and the choice architecture just does not affect them.

Or consider this one:

In a large community of choosers, some shoppers choose particular kinds of bread, no matter where the bread is placed. They are well-informed; they happen to like those kinds of bread. In terms of what they care about, they are not relevantly different from other people, in their community, who are highly susceptible to nudges and who are happy, after the fact, whether or not they are nudged.

It is both tempting and plausible to think that in cases of this kind, we have an excellent way out of our dilemma—one that respects freedom and promises to promote well-being. We should follow the judgments of choosers who are at once informed and consistent! The reason is that such choosers are in an excellent position to know what is best. Choice architects should develop a design to ensure that inconsistent choosers, or those who are susceptible to being nudged, end up taking their guidance from consistent choosers, or those who are not susceptible to being nudged. On this approach, choice architects are comparatively modest. They act on the basis not of their own assessments, but the assessments of choosers whom they have reason to trust.

Well-being, directly

That approach sounds reasonable, but there is another option. It would focus directly on people's well-being. It would not make the choices of informed people authoritative, even if they are free and consistent. Simply for purposes of exposition, we can associate this approach with the great utilitarian thinker Jeremy Bentham. (I do not mean to suggest that Bentham would have endorsed this approach, or that the criterion for well-being must be narrowly utilitarian.[9]) On what I am calling the Benthamite approach, the question is *which approach really does promote people's well-being, suitably defined.*

This approach imposes more serious burdens on choice architects. It requires them to ask and answer the well-being question, rather than to identify and track the behavior of informed choosers. It requires them to engage challenging normative and empirical issues. In cases of transformative experiences, those issues are especially difficult, because we have to ask what kind of life is best.

Consider a relatively mundane case:

Banks in Los Angeles offer "overdraft protection programs," which provide that if customers overdraw their checking accounts, they can still receive the money, paying a high interest rate. Some banks in Los Angeles offer "opt out" programs: They automatically enroll customers into overdraft protection programs, while allowing them to opt out. Other banks in Los Angeles have "opt in" programs: They do not automatically enroll customers but require them to "opt in" (and encourage them to do so). Many customers seem to be both consistent and informed: Whatever the design, they enroll in overdraft protection programs. Many other customers, not evidently different from the consistent group, seem nudgeable: Whether they enroll depends on the default rule.

Or consider this one:

Some high school cafeterias are arranged so that the tastiest foods—brownies, cakes, ice cream—are quite visible and prominent.

Other cafeterias, in other high schools, are arranged so that the healthiest foods—fruits and vegetables—are quite visible and prominent. The choices of many students are a product of the arrangement: What they select depends on what is most visible and prominent. Those students are nudgeable. But the choices of many other students, not evidently different from the nudgeable group, are consistent and apparently informed. They select the tastiest foods, whatever the arrangement.

The consistent choosers in the two cases end up in overdraft protection programs and with brownies, cakes, and ice cream. It is not at all clear that in either case, the best approach is to follow the consistent choosers. The reason is that such choosers might be making big mistakes. In the case of overdraft protection, people might be deciding to take out high-interest loans when a little self-discipline would make that unnecessary. In the cafeteria case, students might be suffering from present bias. A healthy nudge might be a terrific idea.

The most general question is how to choose between the Millian approach (following the consistent, informed choosers) and the Benthamite approach (making an independent judgment about what promotes people's well-being). The ultimate criterion must be Benthamite, which is to say that human well-being is what matters. But that does not at all mean that the Benthamite approach enjoys an easy victory.

Suppose we think that consistent, informed choosers know what they are doing. Suppose we insist that because they are consistent and informed, we really can trust them. Suppose finally that choice architects, trying to decide what approach would promote people's well-being, would make plenty of mistakes. Perhaps they do not know enough. Perhaps their motivations are not pure. On those assumptions, we would do well to follow Mill.

In some contexts, those assumptions are the right ones. But not in all contexts. Choosers might be informed and consistent, but they might suffer from a behavioral bias, such as unrealistic optimism or present bias. Their own choices might not promote their well-being. Choice architects might be trustworthy, or at least trustworthy enough. If so, they should not follow the choices of informed, consistent choosers. By hypothesis, they know better.

Some cases are relatively mundane on this count; knowledge of facts is enough. The cases of George, Diane, and Thomas are arguable examples. Some cases are harder, especially when we are dealing with large groups or populations. Choosers may respond in diverse ways, so that some are more satisfied after they have been nudged, and others are not. (Changing jobs or locations may be like that.) Now add the potential difficulty in deciding what makes people's lives go well. In some ways, it might be better to follow path X, but in other ways, path Y might be better. Some meals are more delicious but less also healthy; some jobs are more fulfilling but also more demanding; some cities are more lively and full of opportunities, but also more stressful (and less navigable). What then?

Once we specify the problem and assemble plenty of facts, we might know the answer. On reasonable factual assumptions, the healthier cafeteria is better, especially if we emphasize that people who really like brownies and cake can find a way to get them. When populations are diverse, we need to know something about how many people can be found in different groups, and also how much they care about the choices in question. Suppose that most people really do prefer overdraft protection programs and that they greatly benefit from them. If so, we have good reason to allow and promote automatic enrollment. But if most people lose from such programs, we might forbid, and certainly not promote, automatic enrollment.

It is important to note that for those who are designing choice architecture, some cases are easy while others are hard. Educative nudges, promoting people's capacity for agency, might be best.[10] So long as freedom of choice is maintained, the stakes are much lower than they would otherwise be. People can go their own way.

COERCION

Turn now to one final topic: coercion.

When there are negative externalities or "harm to others," coercion might be justified;

but let us put that possibility to one side. Might people's freedom of choice fail to promote their own well-being? Every member of the human species knows that the answer is sometimes yes. If people suffer from unrealistic optimism, limited attention, or a problem of self-control, and if the result is a serious injury to well-being, there is an argument for some kind of mandate. To see the argument, let us engage a somewhat technical question: whether to mandate fuel economy standards for automobiles. If the question seems too technical, we can take the analysis as a basis for exploring other questions, such as whether to ban smoking, to mandate savings, to forbid boxing, or to impose cigarette, alcohol, or soda taxes.

It is true that fuel economy standards reduce air pollution, and to that extent help control externalities. But the preferred response to externalities is a corrective tax, not a mandate, and in any case, aggressive fuel economy standards impose high costs (in the form of more expensive vehicles). True, the benefits, in terms of reductions in air pollution and other externalities, are also very high. But at least in the United States, those benefits do not come close to justifying the costs of recent requirements (imposed by the Obama administration but under reconsideration by the Trump administration). What justifies the regulations, according to the government itself, are the *economic savings to consumers*. In other words, fuel economy mandates give consumers big savings (lower costs of operating vehicles, because of lower overall gasoline costs, and also time saved) that end up justifying the costs. If we do not count those benefits to consumers, aggressive fuel economy standards would be hard to defend, because the costs would exceed the benefits.[11]

But should the benefits to consumers be counted? Why can't consumers make their own decisions about which vehicles they prefer? After all, fuel-efficient vehicles are available, and many consumers just don't want them. Why should government require people to get vehicles that they seem not to want?

If the answer is that consumers lack information, the freedom-preserving approach, associated with Mill, is simple: Tell consumers about the savings in terms of both money and time. In this context, however, there is a serious risk that such a nudge will be inadequate. Even with the best fuel economy label in the world, consumers might well be insufficiently attentive to those savings at the time of purchase, not because they have made a rational judgment that they are outweighed by other factors, but simply because most of their focus is on other variables. (How many consumers think about time-savings when they are deciding whether to buy a fuel-efficient vehicle?)

If so, a suitably designed fuel economy mandate—hard paternalism, and no mere nudge--might end up producing an outcome akin to what we would see if consumers were at once informed and attentive. Suppose that the benefits of the mandate greatly exceed the costs. and that there is no significant loss in terms of consumer welfare (in the form, for example, of reductions in safety, performance, or aesthetics). If so, there is good reason to believe that the mandate does make consumers better off. Freedom of choice fails. And if that is true for the question of fuel-efficient cars, it might be true in a wide range of cases in which people are making choices that do not, on balance, promote their own well-being.

We should be cautious before accepting that conclusion. Behavioral biases have to be demonstrated, not simply asserted; perhaps most consumers do pay a lot of attention to the benefits of fuel-efficient vehicles. The government's numbers, projecting costs and benefits, might be wrong. It is important to emphasize that consumers have diverse preferences with respect to vehicles, and regulation might end up decreasing consumers' access to vehicles with attributes that many of them prefer. Despite these qualifications, the argument for fuel economy standards, made by reference to behavioral market failures, is at least plausible. In this context, nudges (in the form of an improved fuel economy label) and mandates (in the form of standards) might march hand-in-hand.

As I have suggested, we could apply the same analysis to many other domains. An obvious one involves savings: Mandatory social security programs, effectively requiring savings, are designed to help people to overcome present bias and self-control programs. They do not allow freedom of choice. Bans on certain drugs (cocaine, heroin) can be understood in similar terms, with the additional point that when people's choices produce an addiction, there is special reason to restrict freedom, which addictions compromise. Cigarette taxes can be understood as an effort to reduce externalities (as from second-hand smoke), but more realistically, they are designed to reduce internalities: the harms that smokers impose on their future selves. Taxes of sugary drinks have the same justification. In the face of what might be treated as an "intrapersonal collective action problem"—seeing people as a series of selves extending over time—a ban or a tax might be justified as a way to improve well-being.

This conclusion raises a final question: When should we depart from the "as judged by themselves" standard? We have seen that if the question is meant to suggest that people's judgments, *before the fact*, are always authoritative, the answer is simple: They are not. People might not welcome a nudge or a mandate even though it is very much in their interests. If the question is whether people's judgments, *after the fact*, might not be authoritative, the answer is less simple. If we are concerned about people's well-being, it is surely relevant, and not at all a good sign, that people reject a mandate or a ban. In a free society, the presumption should be that they are right. But presumptions can be rebutted. If the issue involves serious harm and if the evidence is very clear, we will have to abandon the "as judged by themselves" standard.

Reluctantly, but still.

"THROUGH EDEN TOOK THEIR SOLITARY WAY"

Freedom of choice should be cherished, but cherishing it is hardly enough. Countless interventions and reforms increase navigability, writ large. They enable people to get where they want to go, and therefore enable them to satisfy their preferences and to realize their values. They operate like maps.

Many other interventions and reforms, helping people to overcome self-control problems, are also welcomed by choosers. Such interventions increase navigability and promote freedom. They can be consistent with the "as judged by themselves" standard. Numerous people acknowledge that they suffer from self-control problems. They welcome the help. They exercise their freedom of choice in its favor.

Sometimes people lack clear preferences. Sometimes their preferences are not firm. When a nudge or other intervention constructs or alters their preferences, and when they would be happy either way, the "as judged by themselves" standard is more difficult to operationalize. It may not lead to a unique solution. But it restricts the universe of candidate solutions, and in that sense helps to orient choice architects. To resolve the most difficult questions, it might make sense to see what informed, consistent choosers do, or instead to make direct inquiries into well-being.

The first approach is best unless choosers suffer from a behavioral bias—and if choice architects cannot be trusted. The second is best if choosers suffer from a behavioral bias—and if choice architects can be trusted. For the future, we need far more careful consideration of the ingredients of well-being, informed by evidence as well as by theory. We need the arts and the humanities, social science, law, and theology.

Some lines from John Milton, in *Paradise Lost*, a tale of freedom, writing about Adam and Eve, who have succumbed to temptation and lost everything, and been expelled by God from the Garden of Eden:[1]

Some natural tears they dropped but wiped them soon;
The world was all before them, where to choose
Their place of rest, and providence their guide;
They hand in hand with wand'ring steps and slow,
Through Eden took their solitary way.

Recall finally the passage from Byatt's *Possession*, also a tale of freedom, of a fortunate fall, and of a uniquely human kind of joy:

In the morning, the whole world had a strange new smell. It was the smell of the aftermath, a green smell, a smell of shredded leaves and oozing resin, of crushed wood and splashed sap, a tart smell, which bore some relation to the smell of bitten apples. It was the smell of death and destruction, and it smelled fresh and lively and hopeful.

ACKNOWLEDGMENTS

In 2018, I was honored to receive the Holberg Prize, and this book is based on the Holberg Lecture, delivered on June 6 in Bergen, Norway. I am more grateful than I can say to the Holberg Committee for its generosity and kindness, and to the audience on that occasion for the same. Particular thanks to Ellen Mortenson, Ole Andreas Sandmo, and Solveigh Stornes for helping to make it such a wonderful visit.

I thank Jacob Goldin, Stephen Greenblatt, L.A. Paul, Lucia Reisch, and Eldar Shafir for valuable comments on earlier versions. Thanks to Maya Bar-Hillel for instructive discussions of the topic of navigability. I am also grateful to Andrew Heinrich, Madeleine Joseph, and

Cody Westphal for excellent comments and research assistance. Many thanks to my editor, Eric Crahan, for terrific guidance and to my agent, Sarah Chalfant, for wisdom and support. Some of these ideas were presented to the Department of Philosophy at the University of North Carolina, Chapel Hill, where I received exceptionally valuable help.

Special thanks to the late Edna Ullmann-Margalit, for collaborative work about decision-making that greatly informed this book, and to Richard Thaler, my coauthor on all things related to nudges and nudging.

In some places, I have drawn on Cass R. Sunstein, *"Better Off, as Judged by Themselves": A Comment on Evaluating Nudges*, 64 Int'l Rev. Econ. 1 (2018), and I am grateful to Robert Sugden for raising some puzzles that helped lead to the exploration here.

NOTES

INTRODUCTION. BITTEN APPLES

1. See Shahram Heshmat, *Addiction: A Behavioral Economic Perspective* (New York: Routledge, 2015); Nick Heather and Gabriel Segal, eds. *Addiction and Choice: Rethinking the Relationship* (New York: Oxford University Press, 2017).

2. *Genesis* 3:6. A superb treatment is Stephen Greenblatt, *The Rise and Fall of Adam and Eve* (New York: W. W. Norton, 2017).

3. A. S. Byatt, *Possession* (New York: Vintage, 1990), 551.

4. John Stuart Mill, *On Liberty* (New York: Dover Thrift Editions, 2002). A careful recent discussion is B. Douglas Bernheim, "The Good, the Bad, and the Ugly: A Unified Approach to Behavioral Welfare Economics," 7 *Journal of Benefit-Cost Analysis* 12, no. 1 (2016): 1–57. By the liberal philosophical tradition, I mean to include a very large number of thinkers, including political conservatives. A critique of Mill, representative of some distinctly

conservative thinking, can be found in James Fitzjames Stephen, *Liberty, Equality, Fraternity* (London: Smith, Elder & Co.; 1874; Ann Arbor, MI: Liberty Fund, 1993). It should be clear that in emphasizing the centrality of navigability, I am bracketing some conceptual issues with respect to the definition of freedom and building on understandings that are (I hope) widely shared.

5. Richard H. Thaler and Cass R. Sunstein, *Nudge: Improving Decisions about Health, Wealth, and Happiness* (New York: Penguin, 2009), 5. An instructive discussion, which repays careful reading but with which I do not fully agree, is B. Douglas Bernheim and Dmitry Taubinsky, "Behavioral Public Economics," NBER Working Paper No. 24828, National Bureau of Economic Research, Cambridge, MA, July 2018, available at http://www.nber.org/papers/w24828.

6. Objections can be found in Sarah Conly, *Against Autonomy* (New York: Cambridge University Press, 2011).

CHAPTER 1. WHAT THE HELL IS WATER?

1. "David Foster Wallace, In His Own Words," *The Economist*, 1843, https://www.1843magazine.com/story/david-foster-wallace-in-his-own-words.

2. Meghan R. Busse et al., *Projection Bias in the Car and Housing Markets*, NBER Working Paper No. 18212,

National Bureau of Economic Research, Cambridge, MA, July 2012, http://www.nber.org/papers/w18212.

3. See Gregory Martin and Ali Yurukoglu, "Bias in Cable News: Persuasion and Polarization," *American Economic Review* 107, no. 9 (2017): 2565–2599.

4. See Steve Krug, *Don't Make Me Think Revisited: A Common Sense Approach to Web and Mobile Usability* (San Francisco: New Riders, 2014).

5. See Mark Whitehead, Rhys Jones, Rachel Lilley, Jessica Pykett, and Rachel Howell, *Neuroliberalism* (New York: Routledge, 2018); David Halpern, *Inside the Nudge Unit* (London: W. H. Allen, 2015); Cass R. Sunstein, *Simpler: The Future of Government* (New York: Simon & Schuster, 2013).

6. Raj Chetty, John N. Friedman, Søren Leth-Petersen, Torben Heien Nielsen, and Tore Olsen, "Active vs. Passive Decisions and Crowdout in Retirement Savings Accounts: Evidence from Denmark," *Quarterly Journal of Economics* 129, no. 3 (2014): 1141–1219; Richard H. Thaler, "Much Ado About Nudging," Behavioral Public Policy Blog (June 2, 2017), https://bppblog.com/2017/06/02/much-ado-about-nudging/.

7. Sumit Agarwal, Souphala, Chomsisengphet, Neale Mahoney, and Johannes Stroebel, "Regulating Consumer Financial Products: Evidence from Credit Cards," *Quarterly Journal of Economic* 130, no. 1 (2014): 111.

8. Friedrich Hayek, *The Road to Serfdom* (London: Routledge Press, 1944): 38–39.

9. See Schlomo Benartzi et al., "Should Governments Invest More in Nudging?" *Psychological Science* 28, no. 8 (2017): 1041–1055.

10. Richard H. Thaler & Cass R. Sunstein, *Nudge: Improving Decisions about Health, Wealth, and Happiness* (New York: Penguin Group, 2009), 5 (italics in original).

11. John Stuart Mill, *On Liberty* 8 (New York: Dover Thrift Editions, 2002) (1859). See B. Douglas Bernheim, "The Good, the Bad, and the Ugly: A Unified Approach to Behavioral Welfare Economics," *Journal of Benefit-Cost Analysis* 7, no. 1 (2016): 1–57, for helpful discussion.

12. Friedrich Hayek, *The Collected Works of F. A. Hayek*, Vol. 15: *The Market and Other Orders*, ed. Bruce Caldwell (Chicago: University of Chicago Press, 2014), 384. For some questions about this claim and also Mill's, see Sarah Conly, *Against Autonomy* (New York: Cambridge University Press, 2011); Cass R. Sunstein, *Why Nudge?* (New Haven, CT: Yale University Press, 2015). I am bracketing those questions here.

13. For discussion, see Cass R. Sunstein, *The Ethics of Influence* (New York: Cambridge University Press. 2016); George Akerlof and Robert Shiller, *Phishing for Phools* (Princeton: Princeton University Press, 2015).

14. I am bracketing here some questions about whether we would object to manipulation if it ends up promoting

people's welfare and if they are happy with what happened, after the fact. For relevant discussion, see Jonathan Baron, "A Welfarist Approach to Manipulation," *Journal of Marketing Behavior* 1, no. 3–4 (2016): 283–291.

15. We might also wonder about cases of diminished capacities. Suppose that people's mental or physical capacities are reduced, but they believe themselves to be better off for one or another reason. Their own judgment might not be authoritative. I do not discuss this problem in detail, because it is hard to identify nudges that diminish people's capacities.

16. Aldous Huxley, *Brave New World* (London: Chatto & Windus, 1932), xii.

17. Huxley, *Brave New World*, 163.

18. Ibid.

CHAPTER 2. NAVIGABILITY

1. Jim Bennett, *Navigation: A Very Short Introduction* (Oxford: Oxford University Press, 2017), 1.

2. See Susan Parker, "Esther Duflo Explains Why She Believes Randomized Control Trials Are So Important," Center for Effective Philanthropy, June 23, 2011, http://cep.org/esther-duflo-explains-why-she-believes-randomized-controlled-trials-are-so-vital/.

3. See Louise Locock et al., "Using a National Narrative of Patient Experience to Promote Local Patient Centered

Quality Improvement: An Ethnographic Process Evaluation of 'Accelerated' Experience-Based Co-Design," *Journal of Health Service Research & Policy* 19, no. 4 (2014): 200–207.

4. See the brilliant discussion of "admin" in Elizabeth Emens, *Life Admin* (Boston: Houghton Mifflin Harcourt, 2019).

CHAPTER 3. SELF-CONTROL

1. See Franz Kafka, "Reflections on Sin, Pain, Hope and the True Way," in *The Great Wall of China: Stories and Reflections* (New York: Schoken, 1970), 87.

2. See Heather and Segal, eds., *Addiction and Choice: Rethinking the Relationship*.

3. Benjamin Rush, *Medical Inquiries and Observations, Upon A Disease of the Mind* (1812).

4. See Daniel Kahneman, *Thinking, Fast and Slow* (New York: Farrar, Strauss and Giroux, 2011).

5. Byatt, *Possession*, 546.

6. See Jalie A. Tucker et al., "Role of Choice Biases and Choice Architecture in Behavioral Economic Strategies to Reduce Addictive Behaviors," in Heather and Segal, eds., *Addiction and Choice*, 346–364, at 351.

7. Russell Brand, "My Life without Drugs," *The Guardian*, March 9, 2013, https://www.theguardian.com/culture/2013/mar/09/russell-brand-life-without-drugs.

8. Stevie Nicks: "I Used to Carry a Gram of Cocaine in My Boot," YouTube, https://www.youtube.com/watch?v=7GVZYLC2y-M.

9. "Heroin Addicts Speak," *National Geographic,* https://www.youtube.com/watch?v=kOPOK24g9Cc.

10. In a ten-year longitudinal study of factors associated with alcohol treatment use and non-use, a commonly cited reason for not seeking help was that the respondent "did not think anyone could help." K. G. Chartier et al., "A 10-Year Study of Factors Associated with Alcohol Treatment Use and Non-Use in a U.S. Population Sample," *Drug and Alcohol Dependence* 160 (2016): 205–211.

11. See Heshmat, *Addiction*, at 239–259; James G. Murphy et al., "Behavioral Economics as a Framework for Brief Motivational Interventions to Reduce Addictive Behaviors," in Heather and Segal, eds., *Addiction and Choice*, 325–345.

12. See Beth Burgess, "The Blindfold of Addiction," in Heather and Segal, eds., *Addiction and Choice*, 307–324, at 307. A helpful discussion of addiction, freedom, and choice can be found in Nick Heather, "Addiction as a Form of Akrasia," in Heather and Segal, eds., *Addiction and Choice*, 133–150, at 133.

13. Friedrich Hayek argued that socialist planners inevitably lack the dispersed knowledge that goes into market prices. See Friedrich Hayek, "The Uses of Knowledge in Society," *American Economic Review* 35, no. 4 (1945): 519–530. I am suggesting an analogy: The planner, at

Time 1, will lack the information held by the doer at Time 2.

14. An excellent discussion, which has informed my treatment here, is Daniel Read, "Which Side Are You On? The Ethics of Self-Command," *Journal of Economic Psychology* 27, no, 5 (2006): 681–693.

CHAPTER 4. HAPPY EITHER WAY

1. Byatt, *Possession*, 552.
2. William Samuelson and Richard Zeckhauser, "Status Quo Bias in Decision Making," *Journal of Risk & Uncertainty* 1 (1988): 7–59.
3. See Edna Ullmann-Margalit, *Normal Rationality* , ed. Cass R. Sunstein and Avishai Margalit (Oxford: Oxford University Press, 2017).
4. See L. A. Paul, Transformative Experience (Oxford: Oxford University Press, 2015).
5. Byatt, *Possession*, at 309.
6. In this respect I depart from Ullmann-Margalit and Paul, who do not approach the question in this way, and who are speaking of a subclass of the cases on which I am focusing here. To oversimplify: Ullmann-Margalit makes the intriguing suggestion that people simply "opt," which is to say that they choose without evident reasons; Paul points to the importance of new experiences. By contrast, my own approach is insistently welfarist. I am

keenly aware that I cannot engage their powerful arguments in this space.

7. Jacob Goldin, "Which Way to Nudge? Uncovering Preferences in the Behavioral Age," *Yale Law Journal* 125, no. 1 (2015): 1–325, at 226; Jacob Goldin and Nicholas Lawson, "Defaults, Mandates, and Taxes: Policy Design with Active and Passive Decision-Makers," *American Law and Economics Review* 18, no. 2 (2016): 438–462.

8. See Jacob Goldin, "Libertarian Quasi-Paternalism," *Missouri Law Review* 82 (2017): 669–682, from which I have learned a great deal.

9. For valuable discussion of various forms of welfarism, see Matthew Adler, *Welfare and Fair Distribution: Beyond Cost-Benefit Analysis* (New York: Oxford University Press, 2011).

10. See Cass R. Sunstein, "Default Rules Are Better than Active Choosing (Often)," *Trends in Cognitive Science* 21, no. 8 (2017): 600–606.

11. For discussion, see Hunt Allcott and Cass R. Sunstein, Regulating Internalities, *Journal of Policy Analysis and Management* 34, no. 3 (2015): 698–705.

EPILOGUE. "THROUGH EDEN TOOK THEIR SOLITARY WAY"

1. For a brilliant discussion, see chapter 11 of Stephen Greenblatt, *The Rise and Fall of Adam and Eve* (2017).